Summer Feet

poems by
Joy Kirsch

Oh that our hearts could have summer feet
To run on the gravel of life
And not get hurt

CONTENTS

Preface

V.   VELOCITY

Acknowledgments

Preface

Joy's unique voice in the local newspaper's "letters to the editor" column caught my eye back in the 1980's. Her letters were insightful, to the point, often poetic.

Later, at the UWSP Writing Lab, Joy helped students to excel, sharing her love of words.

Her years as a library aide, meant that fellow workers and curious readers alike gained inside information on good books to borrow. Especially poetry. Who knew Joy was writing her own poetry while immersed in helping others?

Joy's friends have also benefited from the poetry she shares at retreats, bookclub, and her yoga classes, as she always has a pertinent poem to read or recite from memory when they would meet.

Lucky for us, Joy wrote and saved the poetry she created over the years.

Now we all can hear her voice.
~*Bobbie Roman*

Summer Feet

I. GLORY BE

GLORY BE

Glory be to the Father and to the Son and to the Holy Ghost
And to the sun and little blue flowers and happy dogs
And chippies with their tails held high

Glory be to the smell of a baby's skin and the feel of the
April sun on your back and the sound of the flicker in the woods
Glory be to the table of friends, to a table of one friend
To your life long friend

Glory be to the dew on a pink petal
An orange sunset
A cloud that takes your breath away

Glory be to water and watermelon
And peach juice that drips off your chin
As it was in the beginning is now and ever shall be
World without end

Amen

ALWAYS KNOCK

It was a hard fast rule in our house
to always knock on a door before you open it.
I did not.
I was a teenager, in a hurry I suppose,
with something I had to address right then and there.
So I opened the door to my parents' bedroom
and with one glance,
I stopped.
And quietly, oh so quietly, closed the door and crept away.

My father, in a most intimate, private moment,
was on his knees, by the side of the bed,
in prayer.

SAVING GRACE

He sits at the table eating the same breakfast saying nothing
Wearing the weight of his depression like the same clothes
He wears every day

The two rabbits out our window, babies, are chasing and playing
One lifts his paw and looks in the window

A fox and her kit, resting on the lawn; the mother licking her baby
like a cat

A woodchuck lumbers across the backyard

The flock of turkeys, the doe with twin fawns

Daily the chipmunks run rapid and squeak when they see me

The tail end of a bee sticks out of a sweet pea blossom

The cardinal, who doesn't know he's red,
Makes me stop and watch until he flies away

The mottled sunlight in the woods, a storm cloud

This precious earth wraps me in its embrace

Lifts me out of his depression

COURAGE

"Speak softly and carry a big stick; you will go far."
    ~Theodore Roosevelt

I saw him in the middle of the road
Just sitting there black and menacing waiting for me

There are always dogs on my walk but this one
I am truly afraid of

It was a choice; go the long way back or go forward

I stop and step into the woods and find a large stick
I walk ahead with wooden courage

We look at each other
He creeps away
I breathe

He's been gone now for years, but I still look for him
Or one like him

There will always be black dogs in your path
Just like there will always be a big stick in the blessed wood

CAN HAIR BE DEPRESSED?

When I was a girl, my mother made me brush my hair
every night before I went to bed – 100 strokes.
It taught me to count and
I was told it would make my hair beautiful...
hair which my grandmother called "my crown of glory."

But I never liked my hair... and

It suddenly occurred to me that my hair is depressed.
For my entire life I have wanted it to be something other
than it naturally is.
I have subjected it to chemicals and heat and rods and pins
and clips and do-dads of all sorts.
I have been embarrassed by it
I have apologized for it
I never appreciated it for what it was

Of course it's depressed

So, in front of everyone, I would like to say
that my hair is straight, not stringy
It's medium brown, not mousy
It's fine, not thin

...and the gray that you see?
That's my "crown of glory."

BUOYS AND GULLS

I stand before the doors
in those cutesy themed restaurants
Mystified

Am I Juliet?
Isolde
Milady
Queen
Eve
Cleopatra

Am I Minnie?
Wonder Woman
Barbie
A Doe
A Squaw
A Hen

Who Am I?
I don't know
I'm just a girl who's gotta go!

A NOTE FROM YOUR GRANDMA

For weeks I've been imagining you
Hanging on by your little fingernails
Do you even have them yet?

Now at the considerable age of four months
I picture you at ease and floating
In your water world

We bless your little beating heart
We wait
We already love you

JANUARY 7, 2015

I was on my way

The car was running
My coat was on
The phone rang

She was gone

Still warm when I arrived

I just missed you I said
I just missed saying goodbye

Would you have heard me?
Did you hear me say Thank You?
Thank You
Thank You

Did you feel my kiss?

Goodbye my only Momma

SEPTEMBER SIXSOME*

We borrow from Grief, a little
Time on the court

Vintage vs. Old Bros
Old Bros vs. 'mom'enators

Instant amazing memories
Creating nostalgia even as we play

Who can forget that day?

When laughter was the linesman
And the score was always
Love Love

*written September 2005 after the funeral of my father

ANOTHER CIRCLE

He led her there to the planted trees,
To the trees in a circle of life.
He led her there in the soft scented woods,
And he asked her to be his wife.

He promised her another ring,
A ring that would sparkle and shine.
This ring of trees is enough she said,
This ring, and the wish to be thine.

II. A CHANGE IN THE WEATHER

A CHANGE IN THE WEATHER

Early January
Ten below
The radio announcer misspeaks
"Today a chance of flowers."

Oh, yes, please...
Give me Pansies and Peonies
Larkspurs and Lilacs
Clouds of Cosmos
Roses and more Roses
Let the petals fall...
Like Rain

ONE FOR THE ROAD

Google says you will be gone soon. Mid September perhaps.
So I get a ladder to reach your feeder, wash it clean, and refill
with the sugary syrup you will need for your flight.

Nature rewards me, as it often does, when I see you
this morning sipping and darting and drinking in flight
Returning time after time.

Yes, my little hummingbird,

May you take a little bit of myself with you as you go.
I give you a little energy, you give me a little energy.

Thank you tiny friend

Safe Journey

I will be here when you get back.

FOURTH OF JULY

With my heart at half mast
I pledge allegiance to the flag
Of the United States of America
And to the republic for which it stands
One nation, everywhere: in Iraq
And Afghanistan
One nation confounded

Mine eyes have seen the glory
Mine eyes have seen the towers topple
The Abu'grab and hooded men
And roadside bombs

Mine eyes have seen enough

One nation, under God, we hope,
With Liberty and Justice for All.

2004

STRING THEORY

I did not know who to ask for help
and remembered that I was promised
strength from You... that all I had to do was ask

I ask now for just a little something to get me through this day
A molecule will do, or an atom
and now I hear there is something even smaller–

A string

Yes, that would be enough
Please give me a little string of your strength
I will tie it around my finger
To remember that I am never alone

AND THE WINNER IS...*

I would like to thank a number of dogs but most of all, Brandy,
Who loved us all unceasingly.
And the squirrel, now long dead, who thought he was burying food
when indeed he planted the tree I love and look at each day.
And I couldn't have gotten through the winter
if it hadn't been for you,
Purple finch and Cardinal.
But most of all, and you know who you are, dear Chickadees
Thanks for the laughs, Chippies,
I forgive you for tunneling under our patio.
Peepers and Cranes, I long for your song each spring,
I can't thank you enough.
Snapping Turtle,
I'm honored that you bury your eggs on our beach.

Yes! I see the 30-second light...

Deer, wild turkeys, ermine, muskrats, woodchuck, beaver, red fox...
It's been a privilege.

Now I know...
You love me, you really love me!

*a nod to Sally Fields 1985 Oscar acceptance speech

9-11-01

Give me permission to cry,
I will fill the oceans

My blood is needed?
I will give it all

And when I am emptied of tears and blood
Fill me up with love, compassion and understanding

Let me see the flower in the crack of the walk
The tiny maple, one leaf turned red

The sun, in its steady grace, sets
On this day of unspeakable carnage
It will also rise on a new day
Full of light and hope and strength

LADY IN WAITING

On 9/11 I cried
Took a long walk
Wrote a poem

I rummaged through a box of souvenirs
And brought her out, the Statue of Liberty
And stood her on my kitchen window sill

She would stand there until the War is over
I silently said.

It's been eleven years and we still wait

There is talk now of a war in another place
I look at her with her lamp held high and want to ask

Lady Liberty, can't you just pick up your skirts and walk away?

ON THIS SUMMER MORNING

The waterbugs are unaware of the drought
and unrest in Syria and the rise of autism.
We cannot see them from a satellite or Google earth.

Backlit by the rising sun,
they look for all the world like little LED lights
on the surface of the pond.

I look down on them swimming
scurrying with seeming purpose and patterns,
grouping and ungrouping, wondering where they are going?
What they are doing besides just being waterbugs.

I wonder how I would look from above,
my scurrying
my wandering
Could anybody make sense of that?

I stand for a long time watching
realizing they don't really have to do anything
in this pond except exactly what they are doing
...reflecting the sun to one another.

September 9, 2012

A CROWDED BOOTH

I take them with me everytime I vote.
It's a bit of a tight fit, with their large hats and full skirts
They sit on each other's laps
The ride is lively with conversation.

In the front seat sits:
Elizabeth Cady Stanton, Lucy Stone, and Susan B. Anthony.

In the back filled to overflowing:
Sojourner Truth
Alice Paul
Lucretia Mott
Sarah and Angelina Grimke
Lucy Burns
Carrie Chapman Catt
Myra Bradwell
and all the unnamed who marched and picketed,
went on hunger strikes, were arrested and jailed,
wrote essays, spoke out for democracy and liberty.

I vote to honor them
All those who came before me, so that today I can have:
social
economic
legal
and political equality.

In this crowded booth with a black marker, I pen my thanks.

III. PONY POST

PONY POST

If you are going to break up with me,
Would you please send
The 'Dear John' letter via pony express?

I know the riders will have to change horses,
Stop to get something to eat, perhaps go to
The outhouse, and do they ever sleep?

Maybe by the time it gets to me, you would
Have tweeted me and told me to ignore that pony.

THE GIFT

Oh, you shouldn't have
I really wish you wouldn't have
It's much too extravagant for me

I never would have thought it
I never would have bought it
For I honestly don't like it, you see

IN MOURNING

It was her trademark in a way...
My friend who wore black everyday.

Could never figure out why...
She didn't give colors a try.

I see in the paper her husband is dead...
Guess that's why I saw her in red.

GROWING UP

I first heard the word "fuck" on a sidewalk in New York State.
"It's what your parents did to make you," Jimmy Murray said.

It was the same year Camille and I wondered how babies came
out of our belly-buttons and we pulled down our pants
in front of the boys.

We clamped roller skates on our shoes, the key around our neck
on a shoelace.
We rode bikes, made forts and hung in trees.
We played Kick the Can and Hide 'n Seek and
Red Rover Red Rover – come over come over – until

Simon Said "take one giant step."

And we did.

MANNERS

He always walked on the curbside when I was with him,
switching when we made a turn.

"You always keep a lady on the inside away from dirt and mud,"
he explained with a grin.
Of course there are no horse drawn wagons anymore, but he
did it anyway, just as he always opened every door for me.

Always took the grocery bags from my arms,
Always made sure I had a place to sit.
Would never think of wearing a hat indoors,
Until he lost his hair to radiation and his head was cold.

Now he struggles with a walker and can lift nothing.

Today I push him in a wheelchair away from the curbside,
Away from all that would harm him.

MERCY

On my way to town
one of those death defying squirrels crossed the road
in front of me.
I clutched the steering wheel willing myself not to veer,
to trust that it would navigate, calculate,
the speed, the breadth of my wheels to avoid a collision.
I look in the rear view mirror and see nothing and sigh.

Another miracle on my way to town.

I remember the rabbit when I was eight.
My father driving; hit a rabbit and looked in the rear view mirror,
And saw movement. He stopped, got out and looked,
got back in the car and said, "I ran over its legs, but it's still alive."
To my query of "What'll we do, Dad?"
he simply and silently backs up
and runs over it again.
It was just the slightest bump,
a tiny little bump that made me weep
in the back seat of my father's car.

ALL BUT ONE

He had a great name, my great-great-grandfather

Thomas Oliver Tiffany
A private in the army of the North
A letter home–I saw it once–
Tells how disappointed he was
Ordered to stay back from his unit
To care for the sick

Because he missed the Battle of Gettysburg
I can sit here 142 years later
And write these words

2005

FOREVER AND EVER

Soldiers grace my family tree
In Revolutionary garb, a Minuteman
A private in Northern Blue at Gettysburg
Army green in '45, their sepia portraits
Upright on my Grandmother's marble tables
Uncles never quite the same for having been there
I was taught to pray for the 'boys in Korea'
Loved one in Vietnam
Think daily of those in Iraq

Ripeness falling
Breaking of branches

Endless waste

COMPASSION

Great-Grandma would giggle when she did it,
Embarrassed a little; making fun of herself
While she held the hose, watering the rocks.

"They look so hot," she'd say, on this summer day,
So long ago.
She always did it and we always laughed.

Yesterday my little granddaughter, helping me water the flowers,
Asked if she could water the rocks too.
So polite to ask and unaware.
I turned my head to hide my tears.
"Of course you may," I said
"No one has watered them for a long time..."

OVERLOAD

Dear God,
I know you're busy
But if you could spare a moment,
I mean, after you listen to the
Hundreds of politicians running for office
Thousands of players and spectators in
Sporting events and people taking off in airplanes
Millions engaged in the Wars of the World
Victims and Orphans of AIDS
And, oh, yeah, the Sudanese watching
Their children die.
And after you cast a watchful eye on my dad
And get Michele back to her family,
Could you please make the sun shine on PaddleQuest?
Thanks

August 10, 2004

IV. AT THE HEART OF IT

AT THE HEART OF IT

I saw him at the post office
This husband of someone I know

Not well, but enough to know that
He has an artificial heart

As I stand behind him in line, I see
He is wearing a pack slung over one shoulder
...the battery that keeps him alive

Here he is, doing a simple errand at the post office
Wearing his heart on his sleeve

A BUDDHA SUTRA: This is because That is

A chair is because of a tree
Because of a carpenter

A warm shower is because of the well
Because of the plumber

Bread is because of the grain
Because of the farmer

A song is because of the notes
Because of the artist

A poem is because of the words
Because of a feeling
Because of the heart

UPLIFTED IN MINNEAPOLIS

I could have missed them
Could have turned another corner
Gone down another street in this city
But I didn't

I wandered onto a path, to a park, to a pond
In time to see them
Eight geese full abreast like one giant wing
Flying toward me, webbed feet outstretched
Landing, splashing in unison
Into my soul

PRETEND

She's a thyroid storm

A raging fever

A babe unborn

A diabetic coma in the middle of the night

A schizophrenic frenzy... a hopeless sight

A compound fracture

A poisoning, a shock

Cardiac failure, complete heart block

Grade 5 cancer

Tumors galore

Grand Mal seizure

Need I say more?

She's hemorrhaging and losing life
Look at her

She's your wife

TEMPTATION

I know it's in there

No matter where I am in the house

I can hear the muffled cry

Begging me to let it out

To set it free on the kitchen counter

To soften

To feel the familiar curve of it's favorite scoop

I hear it call to me

From the freezer

The half gallon

of

Toasted Almond Fudge

IN THE KITCHEN

On days like this
I feel as if my feet will grow roots–
They inch to the ground
Wrapping themselves around floorboards
And joists

My hands are cleansed in an endless sink of dishes
Wiping counters so often there is no longer a pattern

I stand there rooted–
Growing old
Hair whitening
Skin sagging
Standing there
Until I fall in a heap

...a rag still in my hands

ON THE DAY YOU WERE BORN

The night before you were born,
We sat in a theater watching Superman
You, moving and kicking, getting ready to fly into this world.
I remember the white billowing smoke and cold
surrounding me as I got into the car that January morning.

What is not written is your Dad right there by my side in awe
Your Dad telling me I made beautiful babies
What is not written is how your brother and especially your sister
couldn't take their eyes off of you
couldn't keep from touching you
Your sister putting her finger in your mouth when you cried,
your own living pacifier
What is not written is the absolute Joy you brought into our lives
that cold January morning.

Happy Birthday

For Matthew: 1979

TRANSPORTATION

Music is transportation to the place where you heard the song,
Really heard the song.

I was 14 years old as I walked through the gym and a boy,
my "wished-for boyfriend," was playing "Ebb Tide" on the piano.
I am in Endicott, New York.

When I hear "Age of Aquarius" I am in Elmhurst, Illinois
walking up the stairway
with my two year old son in my arms.

When Louis Armstrong sings "What a Wonderful World"
I am on a boat in the Apostle Islands
making blueberry pancakes on a summer morning.

Recently with earbuds, walking up the driveway,
 a song stopped me in my tracks.
I listened, and there I was again in a 1970 Camaro.

At three months, he was tiny and fit inside a hand towel
 I held between my legs
as I walked to the car to go to the hospital.

I lay on the back seat and my husband drove,
one hand on the steering wheel,
one hand stretched out behind, holding mine.
He had the radio on
Debbie Boone sang: "You Light Up My Life."

He would be 40 this year

2017

MATH

You are 6
I am 72

I may be able to climb up on a bleacher seat
At your high school graduation
I will be 84

I may miss your wedding
I will certainly miss your children

But maybe I can meet the man you will become
When I am 92

I hate leaving before it's over
I never choose to leave a play at intermission.

April 2014

LITTLE BABY

Do you know what you did?

You arrived and changed us all:

Mere mortals became parents

You put the Grand in Mother

You made Aunts and Uncles

Cousins and a Sister

You don't even know the word Love

And yet you embody it in your chubby folds

A magic trick by a lightweight

~Maceo, 2014

TO MY DAUGHTER

How easily your little daughter accepts me
She holds your hand as she goes upstairs to bed
Then stops and turns and looks back at me

"Well, come on, Gramma."
She invites me into her world, into her family

An invitation without precedence

Imagine

I get to love you all over again

FOR MADELIN

Here comes Santa Claus

The Easter Bunny

The Tooth Fairy and Fairy Godmothers

Here comes sleepless nights and

Boundless Joy

Here comes Love

Unbelievable

Unimaginable

Forever

Love

YOUR BABY WILL BE HERE IN THE SPRING

Your baby is waiting in the wet dark warmth
Waiting for form and strength

We wait in the short dark days, cold…
Wrapped in patience and wool

The trees wait for their layer of leaves

The earth waits for sun and seed

The river waits to move again

Winter teaches us
We learn to wait knowing that it will come

Spring

A Baby

Your baby will be here in the Spring

Evelyn was born in 2015

MORE THAN SUPPER

It was two men in a boat
Not needing to talk
Just sitting – with a pole and the hope of a fish

It was the sound of the birds and water lapping
And the silence of expectation

It was the joy of the catch
The job of cleaning
The packaging
The freezing of filets

It was standing in the garage sharing with a neighbor
The thoughtfulness
The taste
The love

So much more than just supper

V. VELOCITY

VELOCITY

As I walk in the wind holding my hat

I think of those reporters standing in the midst of a storm
In their slickers and boots, microphones in hand
Standing up against hurricane force winds.

I think of Sandy Hook Elementary
The finish line at the Boston Marathon
A 3 year old lost in a hotel swimming pool
Cancer that claims a sister, a best friend.

I think of those who stand up as wave after wave hits them
Standing
Miraculously moving forward in tiny little steps
As great gusts of grief slam into them.

Grief that can never be measured.

MUST I KNEEL?

Must I kneel to say a prayer, or can I think of you with my hands
In soapy water scraping scalloped potatoes burned on a dish?

Do I need to go to church and light a votive, or can I light a candle
On the cozy kitchen table and wish you well?

Can I lie in a darkened room
and think of you in an overlit one
with beepers and tubes and strangers attending,
and send healing thoughts?

When I say I am praying for you, is it okay
just to hold you in my heart
while I drive to town?

Must I kneel?

WHERE HAVE YOU GONE?

Where do you go when you go away?
I can see by the look on your face
That wherever you go when you go away
It must be a terrible place

I cannot bear to see your pain, so let me be a part
Take me along when you go again
And I'll guard you with my heart

SUPPORT

I need a cane, a crane
a prop; tall and strong
Pulleys and steel

I need bricks and mortar
prayers and supplications

I am drowning

I need a full face mask
a down blanket wrapped tight
hot brandy, tea and thee

Hold me up

ROMANCE

I dropped them in the Romance section of the public library
My black gloves

I shouldn't have needed them on this late April day
Nor the Romance novel either
But I was cold and lonely

I needed them both

LIGHTEN UP

Won't you add a little sweetness to the coffee of my life?
A smile, a touch, a word of praise...

What are friends for if not to lighten
the bitterness of our daily brew?

I never could drink it black.

HOW ARE YOU?

You like to wear your guise of gloom
Up front for all to see
It keeps your tale of woe alive
And in my company

I like to wear a mask of glee
Pretending all the while
Hiding hurts and sobs within
And calling it a smile

SALMON STEAKS

He drove north to buy that perfect boat,
The Baha Cruiser that needed care and repair.
He heaps the back of the Tahoe with bags and poles
and boxes of lures.
Out on the water, before the sun comes up,
with a McDonalds breakfast in a little white bag.

He brings out the Tackle!
The downriggers, dodgers, spoons, flashers, J-plugs, herring-
The radio chirps with news of The Fish:
Where are they?
How deep?
What color will they hit this morning?

Snagged in the belly, it takes two hours to bring it in.
Is this the one that sits on our plates?
Neat little steaks marinated and grilled to perfection.
Is this a Coho?
A King?
This is effort. This is love and sport.
This is dinner.

TUESDAY'S MAIL?

It's there somewhere
Buried deep in piles untouched

Supper?
Crack a can or slice some cheese
Could you answer the phone please?

Recycling?
Take it down if you wish
Actually, I don't care what you do...

I'm going to bed.

I've got the flu.

ON YOUR WEDDING DAY

For your journey, I could not find a map,

for each marriage is a country unto itself

complete with its own language
vast terrain
and lakes of unfathomable depth.

What advice can I give but to
pack that which you already have:
Honesty
Compassion
Creativity
Fill up with Gratitude

Hold each other tight through the curves
Brace yourself for the ruts
and know that at each overlook
you will be able to turn to your best friend and say
Oh, Honey
Isn't it beautiful?

For Lorelei and Harlow
October, 2006

CONNECTION

I didn't care how I looked
Wearing my old teal coat
A visor for the sun...Anne's old holey hat atop

It's just a walk along the same road
and we are friends
this road and I
It has heard all I have to say

I gladly dodge puddles today
this March melting day
as I wait and walk to Spring

I stop at the mailbox and see the manila mailer
...the Amherst address, the name of the poet
I hold it close
Smile
Walk with care up the icy drive
Finding bare asphalt so as not to slip

I hang up my coat, remove my shoes, draw a drink of water
Sit at the table in front of a vase of daffodils
The sun warming the room
Only then do I open my gift and feel how it feels to connect
And be touched by another
with only words.

In Memoriam to poet Pat Schneider 1934-2020

ACKNOWLEDGMENTS

I wish to thank Madelin Petz and Lorelei MacBeth for encouraging me to publish this book. Without their editing and organizational skills, I could not have finished this project which means so much to me. Thank you.

To Jim Pollock who chaired our writing group and all the supportive members of AASP (Aspiring Authors of Stevens Point).

And to my dear friend Bobbie Roman who heard many of these poems during the 25 years we gave each other writing assignments and shared them at our weekly breakfast/lunch dates.

To the editors of the following publications in which some of these poems appeared:

- UWSP Barney Street 2002

- WOW Writers of Wisconsin
  15th anniversary edition 2002

- Wisconsin Poets Calendar:
  2008, 2014 & 2017

- Q Gallery "Verses and Visions"
  2011 & 2012